940.1 O'Brien
Your guide to knights and the
age of chivalry

DESTINATION
Middle Ages

Your Guide to
Knights and the
Age of Chivalry

Cynthia O'Brien

Crabtree Publishing Company
www.crabtreebooks.com

Crabtree Publishing Company
www.crabtreebooks.com

Author: Cynthia O'Brien

Managing Editor: Tim Cooke

Designer: Lynne Lennon

Picture Manager: Sophie Mortimer

Design Manager: Keith Davis

Editorial Director: Lindsey Lowe

Children's Publisher: Anne O'Daly

Editor: Petrice Custance

Proofreader: Wendy Scavuzzo

**Production coordinator
and prepress technician:** Tammy McGarr

Print coordinator: Margaret Amy Salter

Written and produced for Crabtree Publishing Company
by Brown Bear Books

Photographs (t=top, b=bottom, l=left, r=right, c=center):
Front Cover: Library of Congress: tr; **Public Domain:** Heidelberg University l, Selby May br; **Thinkstock:** Photos.com cr.

Interior: 123rf: Valery Sibrikov 22r; **Alamy:** Art Archive 21tl, Chronicle 16l, Patrick Forget/Sagaphoto.com 29b, Granger Collection 27r, Angelo Hornak 8, Interfoto 13bl, Mary Evans Picutre Library 24r, North Wind Picuture Archives 19t, 23r; **Bridgeman Art Library:** 14r, 20bl; **Dreamstime:** Evgeniy Fesenko 9b, Alex Max 17r; **Getty Images:** Ann Ronan Picture Library 11b; **Public Domain:** Adrian Barlandus 10r, Albrecht Durer 21br, Essex Records Office 13r, Hull Historian 24bl, Oregon Education 12, Sailko 5t, Chateau de Versailles 17l, Warsaw, National Museum/NMW 19br; **Shutterstock:** Vladimir Korostyshevskiy 11t,Welcomia 25; SuperStock: 16r; **Thinkstock:** istockphoto 4, Photos.com 5b, 10bl, 26; **Topfoto:** British Library Board 22bl, Fine Art Images/HIP 15, 18, 29t, The Granger Collection 27t, 28, The Image Works 14b, Topham Picturepoint 9tl, Charles Walker 9cr, World History Archive 20r.

All other photos, artwork and maps, **Brown Bear Books**.

Brown Bear Books has made every attempt to contact the copyright holder. If you have any information please contact licensing@brownbearbooks.co.uk

Library and Archives Canada Cataloguing in Publication

O'Brien, Cynthia (Cynthia J.), author
Your guide to knights and the age of chivalry / Cynthia O'Brien.

(Destination: Middle Ages)
Includes index.
Issued in print and electronic formats.
ISBN 978-0-7787-2992-1 (hardcover).--
ISBN 978-0-7787-2998-3 (softcover).--
ISBN 978-1-4271-1865-3 (HTML)

1. Knights and knighthood--Juvenile literature. 2. Chivalry--Juvenile literature. 3. Middle Ages--Juvenile literature. 4. Civilization, Medieval--Juvenile literature. 5. Knights and knighthood--Europe--History--To 1500--Juvenile literature. 6. Chivalry--Europe--History--To 1500--Juvenile literature. I. Title.

CR4513.O27 2017   j940.1   C2016-907393-9
                                         C2016-907394-7

Library of Congress Cataloging-in-Publication Data

Names: O'Brien, Cynthia (Cynthia J.), author.
Title: Your guide to knights and the age of chivalry / Cynthia O'Brien.
Description: New York, New York : Crabtree Publishing, 2017. |
  Series: Destination: Middle Ages | Includes index.
Identifiers: LCCN 2017000081 (print) | LCCN 2017004298 (ebook) |
  ISBN 9780778729921 (reinforced library binding : alkaline paper) |
  ISBN 9780778729983 (paperback : alkaline paper) |
  ISBN 9781427118653 (Electronic HTML)
Subjects: LCSH: Knights and knighthood--Juvenile literature. |
  Chivalry--Juvenile literature. | Middle Ages--Juvenile literature.
Classification: LCC CR4513 .O26 2017 (print) | LCC CR4513 (ebook) |
  DDC 355--dc23
LC record available at https://lccn.loc.gov/2017000081

Crabtree Publishing Company
www.crabtreebooks.com   1-800-387-7650

Printed in Canada/032017/BF20170111

Published in Canada
Crabtree Publishing
616 Welland Ave.
St. Catharines, ON
L2M 5V6

Published in the United States
Crabtree Publishing
PMB 59051
350 Fifth Avenue, 59th Floor
New York, New York 10118

Published in the United Kingdom
Crabtree Publishing
Maritime House
Basin Road North, Hove
BN41 1WR

Published in Australia
Crabtree Publishing
3 Charles Street
Coburg North
VIC, 3058

Contents

Before We Start

The many wars of the Middle Ages were mainly fought by knights on horseback. Knights tried to live by the ideals of chivalry, rules of behavior based on fairness, courage, and honor.

TIMES OF CHANGE

+ Defining the Middle Ages

The Middle Ages is the name given to a period that lasted about 1,000 years, beginning around the end of the Roman Empire in 476. The early Middle Ages lasted until about 1000. The later Middle Ages, which lasted until about 1500, was a time of great **migration** and nation building. Kings built larger kingdoms by taking land from their neighbors, forcing defeated peoples to find new land of their own. Knights took a leading role in the kings' wars of conquest.

THE SHAPE OF EUROPE

☛ Competing empires

In medieval times, Christians ruled much of Europe. The Pope led the Roman Catholic Church. He supported the Holy Roman Empire, which dominated central and western Europe. The Byzantine Empire of present-day Turkey and Greece followed Eastern Orthodox Christianity. Meanwhile, Islamic empires rose in North Africa, the Middle East, and Spain. Christians and Muslims fought over their religions (right), but also over land and power.

THE FEUDAL SYSTEM
✦ Structure of society

In the 900s and 1000s, the **feudal system** shaped society. The king shared land among his lords in return for their support. Each lord granted land to **vassals**. In return, a vassal agreed to be loyal to the lord and supply him with soldiers. By the 1200s, many vassals had become knights. Peasants, or farmers, worked the land (left) for knights in return for being housed, supported, and protected.

TOP OF THE PILE

☛ Nobles and knights...

☛ ...have the power

A strict **hierarchy** existed in the Middle Ages. The king and other **nobles**, such as dukes, were the most powerful people. Peasants had no wealth or power. The first knights (right) did not own land or have high social standing. However, after the **Crusades** began at the end of the 1000s, knights became more important. By the middle of the 1200s, only men of noble birth could become knights. Knights fought for their lord and king. They fought in the Crusades, the battles of the Hundred Years' War, and many other **sieges** and conflicts.

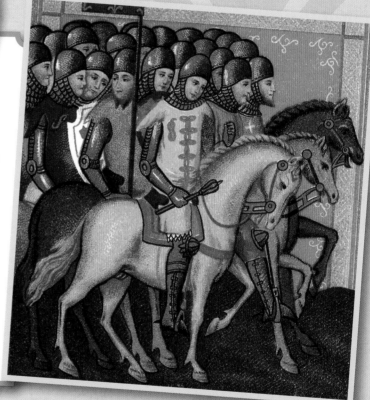

CENTERS OF POWER
✦ My home is my castle

Medieval kings and lords built fortified homes called castles. Castles allowed lords to control the land and people around them. The lord, his family, servants, and knights lived in the castle. Few knights owned castles, but many owned and lived in manor houses. These knights had land and had peasants who worked for them.

Where in the World?

During the Middle Ages, societies around the world had a special group of elite warriors. In Europe, these warriors were called knights, and a code of behavior emerged based on their service to their lords.

England
Some of the most famous medieval knights and rulers came from England. They were important in the Hundred Years' War with France, from 1337 until 1453.

ENGLAND

EUROPE

Bruges

FRANCE

Tours

Poitiers

Poitiers
Eleanor of Aquitaine was born and died in Poitiers. She was queen of France and England at different times. Eleanor's court was a center of European culture, where ideas such as **courtly love** were popular. Courtly love described the way in which a knight fell in love with a lady and performed great deeds in her honor.

SPAIN

Tours
The knights of the Frankish ruler Charles Martel defeated Islamic invaders at Tours in 732. Charles created the feudal system that later became the basis of society in many parts of Europe.

Baltic States

The states of the Baltic were the last part of Europe to become Christian. The Teutonic Knights from Germany went to fight there to force the Baltic peoples to convert to Christianity.

Bruges

The last medieval **tournament** took place at Bruges in 1379. Knights gathered at these meetings to display their fighting skills. Tournaments gradually died out as knights on horseback became less effective on the battlefield than new weapons such as guns.

ISRAEL
Jerusalem

Jerusalem

Jerusalem is holy to Muslims, Christians, and Jews. Muslim armies seized the city from the Byzantine Empire in 637. In the Crusades that began in 1095, European Christians fought a series of campaigns to try to win the city back.

New Names

This map shows the modern names of countries. Most of these states did not exist in the Middle Ages.

Who We'll Meet

Colorful characters inhabited medieval society, from powerful kings and queens to legendary knights and warriors. Many shaped the world in which they lived.

HAMMER OF THE SCOTS

+ **Edward fights the Crusades...**

+ **...conquers Wales and Scotland**

Edward I (right) was king of England from 1272 to 1307. He was known for his skill and courage in battle. Before becoming king, Edward fought in the Crusades in the Holy Land. As king, he brought Wales under English control. In the late 1200s, Edward conquered Scotland and became known as the "Hammer of the Scots." He died in 1307 on his way to fight the Scottish rebel, Robert the Bruce.

WHERE'S THE KING?

✦ **Richard has a lion's heart...**

✦ **...but is rarely at home**

When Richard I became king of England in 1189, he began to raise money for the Third Crusade. In 1190, he traveled to the Holy Land and defeated the Muslims in 1191. Richard failed to win Jerusalem, but he called a **truce** with Saladin, the Muslim leader. In 1196, Richard went to war to protect his lands in France from King Philip II. He was killed in France in 1199. His bravery and military skill won him the nickname "Lionheart." During the 10 years he reigned, Richard was only in England for about six months.

QUEEN OF COURTLY LOVE

✦ **Eleanor rules France...**

✦ **...and then England**

At age 15, Eleanor of Aquitaine became queen of France. She traveled widely with her husband, King Louis VII, but the marriage ended in 1152. Eleanor then married Henry Plantagenet, who later became king of England. When she was older, Eleanor's court at Poitier's was a center of artistic and literary ideas, such as courtly love.

A FAMOUS OUTLAW

☞ **Was Robin Hood real?**

The name Robin Hood (right) first appears in 1377. He is briefly mentioned as an **outlaw** in an English poem called *Piers Plowman*. The story of Robin Hood grew into a famous legend. He is said to have been a knight who fought in the Crusades. When he returned to England, he fought for the rights of the poor with the support of the king, Richard the Lionheart. By the late 1400s, all tales of Robin Hood described him as an honorable outlaw.

Outlaw
There is no evidence that a real Robin Hood ever existed. He was so popular, however, that some real outlaws later called themselves Robin Hood.

NEWS FROM AFAR

Salāh al-Dīn Yūsuf ibn Ayyūb, or Saladin, was the most famous medieval Muslim leader. He ruled Egypt and Syria, and led his army to defeat the crusaders at the Battle of Hattin in 1187. Afterward, Saladin took the city of Jerusalem for the Muslims. Saladin lost some of this land to Richard I during the Third Crusade, but kept control of Jerusalem.

A Little Bit of History

As empires expanded and leaders came and went, tens of thousands of warriors went to war in the name of their lords or their religion. Knights were central figures in the major events of the era.

"THE HAMMER"

+ Charles leads the Franks

+ Muslim advance halted

Charles Martel (right) was a leader of the Franks, who lived in what is now France. After rising to power in about 717, Charles expanded the Frankish empire into Germany. When Muslim raiders from Spain tried to advance into France, Charles and his army of knights defeated them at the Battle of Tours in 732. The victory stopped the Muslim advance into Europe. Charles's grandson, Charlemagne, became the first Holy Roman Emperor in 800.

THE FIRST KNIGHTS

✦ Fighting for the king

Knights first appeared sometime in the 700s. An early feudal system emerged under Charles Martel and then Charlemagne. By the late 1000s, the system was well established. Under Charlemagne and later rulers, knights pledged loyalty not only to their lord, but also to the Christian Church. By the 1200s, knights were not only soldiers. They became wealthy landowners, and important members of medieval society.

RELIGIOUS WARS
✦ Struggle for the Holy Land

The Crusades were a series of wars fought by Christians and Muslims in the Holy Land. In 1095, Pope Urban II called for Christians to conquer Jerusalem. Knights and soldiers answered the call. They believed it was their duty to force Muslims to leave the Holy Land. Eight crusades followed, ending in the defeat of a Christian army in 1270.

NEWS FROM AFAR

In 638, Muslim Arabs captured the city of Jerusalem, which was holy for Christians, Jews, and Muslims. By the early 700s, Muslims controlled Syria, North Africa, and Spain. By the First Crusade in 1095, the Islamic world was larger than the combined Christian empires of Europe.

MY MEDIEVAL JOURNAL

Imagine you are a French soldier in the Siege of Orléans. You realize that the warrior leading you into battle is a young girl. Write a letter describing the effect you think that would have on your companions as you prepare to fight.

ENGLAND VS. FRANCE

☞ Hundred Years' War...

☞ ...lasts 116 years!

The Hundred Years' War lasted from 1337 until 1453. It began when France and England argued over possession of territory in France. In 1429, a peasant girl known as Joan of Arc led French soldiers to victory at Orléans. Joan helped to turn the war in favor of the French. She was later executed (left) by the English. The war ended in 1453, with French victory at Castillon.

Serving the Lord

The main purpose of a knight was to fight. Knights pledged loyalty and service to their lord in wars over territory, between nations, and over religion.

Did you know?

After the 1200s, knights no longer fought in battles. Mounted soldiers still remained key to many armies. They were called cavalry and could move quickly.

SERVING THE LORD

✦ Vassals supply men

Part of a knight's **oath** as a vassal was to supply peasants to fight for the lord. A vassal pledged to fight for 40 days per year, although during wartime he fought as many days as necessary. The size of a lord's various lands and wealth decided how many knights he had in his service. In the early Middle Ages, lords used thousands of knights (right). By the 1200s, English kings raised armies of about 400 knights. Most of the army was made up of foot soldiers, archers, and **mercenaries**.

KINGS IN BATTLE

✦ Leading from the front

According to Geoffroi de Charny's book on chivalry, kings had a duty to be "the first to take up arms and to strive with all their might and expose themselves to the physical dangers of battle in defense of their people and their land." Many medieval kings did lead their armies into battle, including England's Richard I and Henry V, El Cid of Castile, Spain, and France's King Louis IX.

THE FIRST KNIGHT

✦ A royal champion

In England, William the Conqueror began to reward one outstanding knight by giving him the honorary title of King's Champion. Since then, a king's or queen's champion has taken part in English **coronations**. The champion vows to fight anyone who challenges the ruler's right to the throne. Sir John Dymoke performed the service at the coronation of Richard II in 1377. The Dymoke family still takes part in the British coronation ceremony—but not on horseback, as in the past.

BREAKING NEWS

Have you heard about the new tax? Henry II came to the English throne in 1154. He is letting knights out of their obligation to fight by paying scutage, which is paying for a letter that will excuse the knight from service (below). This works in the king's favor. He can then use the money to hire mercenaries to fight for him instead of aging knights. Other kings in Europe are following Henry. They are also using the first **professional** armies.

THE CHANGING FACE OF WARFARE

☛ Gunpowder changes things

Weaponry changed in the later Middle Ages. In the mid 1300s, large numbers of archers used **longbows** to attack the enemy. Foot soldiers began using guns and gunpowder (left), and used cannons in sieges. Knights became less important on the battlefield. They could easily be killed by the new weapons. By the early 1400s, nations were using professional armies. Soldiers using the powerful new weapons replaced knights.

Codes of Chivalry

Chivalry began as a moral **code for knights as warriors. It developed into an** idealized **view of knights and their** adventures that was repeated in poetry and legend.

Song
In *The Song of Roland*, a knight named Roland defends France from Muslims. He blows his horn to summon help, although he knows the enemy will find and kill him.

CODE OF HONOR

+ **Behave yourself!**

+ **...even in battle**

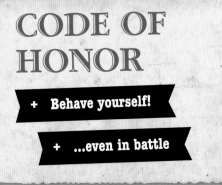

Medieval knights followed a strict code of behavior. This code of chivalry demanded that they be brave, honorable, and loyal. In particular, knights must fight for their king and church, protect the weak, and honor women. Poems such as *The Song of Roland* (right) made chivalry part of medieval culture. Such poems celebrated the deeds of fighting men. However, some modern critics point out that chivalry was based on an idea that women were weak and needed protection, which was often not true.

NOBLE POETS

✦ **Songs of war**

✦ **Songs of love**

Troubadours were noblemen who wrote poems, which they sang out loud, or which **minstrels** sang. Originally from France, troubadours wrote about the heroism and skill of knights. They also wrote many love poems telling stories about knights trying to win the love of a lady. Eleanor of Aquitaine encouraged writers and artists. Troubadours often entertained at her court in France.

AN ORDER OF HONOR

+ The king's companions

Possibly inspired by stories of the legendary King Arthur, King Edward III of England established the Order of the Garter in 1348. The order was based on ideas of chivalry. Edward appointed 25 knights, called "companions," for their loyalty and service. Other royal **orders** followed, such as the Golden Fleece in France. The Order of the Garter continues today. England's monarch is its head, and women and men serve as "knight companions."

MY MEDIEVAL JOURNAL

A quest is a long adventure that leads people into danger, as in the quest for the Holy Grail. Write your own story about someone setting out to achieve something difficult in the modern world, such as getting a ticket for a popular sports or music event.

KNIGHTS OF THE ROUND TABLE

☞ A legendary king

☞ Arthur and Camelot

King Arthur first appeared in *The History of the Kings of Britain*, written in 1136. He was a king who defended Britain against the Saxons in the 400s. There is no evidence that Arthur ever existed, but the stories were **romantic** and exciting. Soon, stories appeared about Arthur's court, Camelot. There, Arthur and knights such as Lancelot and Galahad met around a round table (left).

THE HOLY GRAIL

+ Arthur's quest

+ The ultimate knightly challenge

One of the most famous adventures of King Arthur and his knights was the quest, or search, for the Holy Grail. The Grail refers to the cup that Jesus is said to have used at the Last Supper. According to stories, only the most honorable knight could retrieve the Grail. In this way, chivalry and Christianity were closely linked. In some stories, Sir Galahad succeeds in finding the Holy Grail, but later takes it with him to heaven.

The Crusades

The Crusades were fought between Christians and non-Christians, such as Muslims. For almost 200 years, Europe's knights went to battle for the Church.

THE FIRST CRUSADE

+ **Urban calls high knights**

On November 27, 1095, Pope Urban II announced the launch of the First Crusade (right). The Christian Church wanted to reclaim the holy city of Jerusalem and the surrounding land from the Muslims. The Pope also agreed to aid the Byzantine Empire, which had lost land to the Turkish Muslims. After the Pope's call, thousands of crusaders traveled to the Holy Land to fight.

KINGS ON CRUSADE

✦ **Monarchs take charge**

✦ **King loses life**

A number of European kings went on crusade. Louis VII of France and Conrad III of Germany led the Second Crusade. King Richard I of England led a Third Crusade to recapture Jerusalem. In the final crusades, King Louis IX of France captured Damietta in Egypt, but later lost many men and his own life in a siege at Tunis during the Eighth Crusade.

BREAKING NEWS

The Crusaders are bringing back all sorts of new ideas, goods, and arts from Asia. There are new woven carpets, mirrors, and new foods such as dates (below). There are even new ways of writing numbers, called Arabic numerals. Islamic styles have also influenced a new style of church design, called gothic!

NEWS FROM AFAR

The First Crusade was led by knights and other nobles. It established four "Crusader states" in present-day Israel, Lebanon, Syria, and Turkey. These were the states of Jerusalem, Antioch, Tripoli, and Edessa. The crusaders built castles to protect their new states (left). However, Edessa fell to Muslim forces in 1144, and Saladin captured Jerusalem in 1187. By the end of the 1300s, none of the Holy Land remained under Christian control.

VICTORIES AND DEFEATS

+ Eight Crusades

During 200 years of conflict, Christian armies launched eight major Crusades in the Holy Land. They laid siege to Muslim strongholds, including Antioch in 1097, Tripoli in 1109, and Damascus in 1148. Although the crusaders won some battles, and the Crusader states lasted for a century or more, many thousands of soldiers died. Ultimately, strong Muslim forces seized back the territory the Christians had won, and the Crusades came to an end.

Knightly Orders

In the Crusades, knights fighting for the Christian church were grouped in orders. The orders combined military and religious duties. The knights were "Soldiers for Christ."

Orders

Knightly orders got their name from religious orders. A monastic order was a group of monks or nuns living under the same set of rules.

FIGHTING FOR THE CHURCH

☞ Knights protect pilgrims

The first military-religious orders developed in the Middle Ages. Knights swore to protect **pilgrims** in the Holy Land and to defend the Church there from Muslims. These knights dedicated their services to the Church and agreed to follow strict rules. Like monks, knights took **vows** of poverty, humility, and devotion to the Church.

THE KNIGHTS TEMPLAR

+ Warriors amass wealth...

+ ...pope abolishes them

A French knight, Hugues de Payens, founded the Knights Templar in about 1120. The knights' uniform was a white **tunic** with a red cross. By the early 1300s, the Templars had accumulated great wealth and owned property across Europe. The order ended abruptly when King Philip IV of France accused the Templars of breaking a number of laws, and arrested them all. Pope Clement V condemned the Templars in 1312. He gave their properties to another order of knights, the Hospitallers.

The Knights Hospitaller began as an order that protected the sick and poor in the Holy Land. Its founder, Father Gerard, ran a **hospice** in Jerusalem. As the order grew, it acquired many properties. The knights dressed in black tunics with a white cross, and in time became a powerful military force. The Knights Hospitaller still exist today. The order concentrates on its original purpose—to help those in need.

TEUTONIC KNIGHTS

☞ **Crusades in Europe**

☞ **Converting the pagans**

In 1190, Germans founded the Teutonic Knights. This order of knights fought in the Baltic states. The knights tried to convert the Baltic **pagans** to Christianity. By the early 1400s, the Teutonic Knights ruled much of eastern Europe. However, armed forces from Poland, Lithuania, and Russia defeated the knights in the Battle of Grunwald in 1410 (right). The Teutonic Knights never returned to their former power.

THE CAVELLERAS

✦ **Spain's female knights**

✦ **The Order of the Hatchet**

Although most knights were men, a few orders existed for women. One of these was in Spain. In 1149, the women of Tortosa, Catalonia, helped defend their town from a Muslim attack. In gratitude, Count Raymond Berenger established the Order of the Hatchet for his female knights, known as the "cavelleras."

Around the World

While knights rose to fame in medieval Europe, other warriors around the world also became leaders of their societies. These powerful soldiers also helped to build and defend empires.

Bushido
The samurai followed a code of behavior called "bushido," or "the way of the warrior." Samurai warriors chose death above dishonor.

JAPANESE SAMURAI

☞ **Serving the lord**

☞ **Living for honor**

Samurai were Japanese warriors who served feudal lords called *daimyos*. Samurai rose to power in the 1100s and became part of Japan's ruling class, known as *shoguns*. Being a samurai was a great honor and privilege, and fathers passed the position down to their sons. Samurai were the only members of society allowed to carry swords. They wore elaborate, colorful armor and fought on horseback (right).

SLAVE SOLDIERS

+ **Mamluks fight for sultan...**

+ **...then take his place**

The name "mamluk" comes from an Arabic word that means "owned." The Mamluks (left) were slaves who trained as soldiers for Muslim leaders. In Egypt, the Mamluks took control after the death of the sultan in 1249. They expanded their power to rule over Egypt and Syria until 1517.

NEWS FROM AFAR

By the 1400s, the Aztecs ruled a large empire in present-day Mexico. Aztec boys trained in battle skills from an early age. They learned how to fight with sharp stone knives and spears. Aztec warriors painted their faces and wore clothing according to their rank. Men from noble families became eagle or jaguar warriors. Eagle warriors wore feathers, while jaguar soldiers wore animal skins (left).

> " *A King maketh his son a Knight, and if the son have no father alive then the next of kin maketh him a knight.* "

English courtier Sir Henry Cristall describes the Gallowglass in Ireland, 1395

FEARSOME SCOTS

+ **Warriors in Ireland**
+ **Soldiers paid to fight**

In the 1100s, Scottish mercenaries arrived in Ireland to fight on behalf of powerful Irish lords. These soldiers were the Gallowglass (right), from a Gaelic word meaning "young foreign warriors." The Gallowglass moved to Ireland as clans, or family groups, and fought under their own leaders. In battle, Gallowglass wore chain mail shirts and carried long battle-axes.

Equipment and Weapons

Being a knight was an expensive profession. Knights bought their own armor, weapons, and horses. They also bought equipment for the men who served them.

BREAKING NEWS

Plate armor is what the wealthiest knights are wearing these days. They used to wear hauberks, or chain-mail tunics. Chain mail was made from metal rings linked together. It did not offer enough protection, so knights are beginning to wear armor made from pieces of metal. Plate armor covers their bodies from top to bottom. The armor weighs about 50 pounds (23 kg). It is not comfortable, but at least they can still move around—barely!

THE FOOT SOLDIERS

✦ It's ok, we'll walk...

Mounted knights sometimes fought on foot, but most fighting on foot was done by infantry, or foot soldiers, and archers. In the early Middle Ages, most of these soldiers were untrained peasants. They defended the knights while the knights prepared to charge the enemy on their horses. By the later Middle Ages, foot soldiers were well-trained professionals armed with longbows and guns.

MIND YOUR HEAD!

✦ **Variety of helmets**

✦ **Visor improves vision**

The most important part of any knight's armor was his helmet. Early medieval knights wore bowl-shaped helmets that covered the tops of their heads. Side and front pieces were later added to protect the ears and nose. In the 1200s, the Great Helm covered the entire head. By the 1300s, knights were wearing *bascinets*, which were helmets with a chain mail collar to protect the neck. The bascinet had a moving visor, which knights raised for better vision when not in combat.

CHARGE!

+ **Knights ride into battle**

+ **Warhorses wear armor**

Knights rode to battle and charged at their enemies on horseback (right). Wealthy knights owned the best warhorses, which were only used in battle. By the late 1100s, these specially trained horses started wearing armor. Each knight owned about four horses for himself and more horses for his squire, or attendant.

My Medieval Journal

Imagine you are a medieval knight going into battle. Which weapons do you think would be most useful to carry? Use the pictures in this book to learn about different medieval weapons. Make lists of the advantages and disadvantages of each.

WEAPONS FOR BATTLE

☞ **Points and blades...**

In battle, a knight carried a shield decorated with his **coat of arms** for protection (right). Knights also carried weapons such as a sword and lance, which is a long pole with a sharp, metal end. Knights charged at the enemy holding the lance. Some knights also carried a battle-ax and a mace, which is a club with a ridged or spiked head.

Life as a Knight

Becoming a knight took many years and a lot of training. When they were not at war, knights were important figures in the community. Most knights came from wealthy families, and many owned land.

STARTING YOUNG

+ Pages serve nobles...

+ ...but receive little education

At age seven, sons of nobles would begin training for knighthood. Called pages, the boys left home to live with another lord at his manor or castle. Pages received basic education, but they also had many chores. They served at banquets and carried messages for the lord and lady. As they grew older, pages learned skills, such as how to use a sword, and how to ride and look after a horse (right).

BREAKING NEWS

Have you got a coat of arms? Since the early 1100s, knights have used designs on their shields to identify themselves. Two hundred years later, there are all sorts of strict rules for creating these coats of arms (left). The rules are called heraldry. Knights and other nobles use these arms as a mark of family and status on their clothing, shields, and banners. The term "coat of arms" comes from the tradition of displaying arms on a tunic worn over armor.

RIGHT-HAND MAN

✦ **Squires assist knights...**

✦ **...until they make the grade**

A page became a squire at about age 14. The squire was an important aide for the knight. He looked after the knight's horses, armor, and weapons. He also helped the knight prepare for battle, and sometimes went to battle with him. Some squires became famous for their bravery in helping to protect a knight. A squire's training involved learning how to **joust** and other battle strategies. After four to seven years of service, a squire qualified to become a knight himself in a **dubbing** ceremony.

Dubbing

A squire usually became a knight in a ceremony. The king touched each of the man's shoulders with the flat blade of a sword.

LIFE ON CAMPAIGN

☛ **Living away from home**

In wartime, knights spent many months away from home. They traveled long distances, making camps along the way. Knights lived in tents, but most other soldiers had little or no shelter. Although soldiers carried some supplies with them, they also stole food from homes they passed. Camps were crowded and dirty. They smelled of horses, unwashed soldiers, and cooking. There was constant noise from blacksmiths and other workers who followed the army.

LIFE AT HOME

+ **Local bosses...**

+ **...and providers of entertainment**

At home, knights lived in manor houses or castles. They spent their time training to keep up their skills. They also went to church, hunted, and looked after their land. Some knights were judges in local courts. At night, knights held feasts where entertainers amused the crowd. But knights knew that at any time they might have to leave their families and head off to war again (right).

Training and Tournaments

Being a knight took skill as well as bravery. Over time, young men perfected their horsemanship and battle techniques. They showed off their talents at tournaments.

ONE-ON-ONE

- + **Jousts test skills**
- + **Knight charges knight**

The main event at a tournament was the joust. The joust involved two mounted knights (above, in helmets). The knights charged toward one another, each holding a long, blunt lance. A knight had to knock his opponent from his horse. If both knights stayed on their horses, they charged again. If both knights fell from their horses, they fought on foot.

BREAKING NEWS

If you're a knight getting ready for war, try a tournament! Not only are tournaments training grounds for knights, but they are also becoming a hugely popular sport. A large tournament attracts knights from all over. Expect to find many different types of contests where you can display fighting techniques. Most events are for individual knights, but why not gather a team of knights and enter the mock battle?

HUNTING AND HAWKING

☞ **Knights chase game**

Part of a squire's training was learning how to hunt. Knights and squires hunted animals such as deer, wild boar, and birds. Part of the training included preparing dead animals before they were taken home to be cooked. When squires became knights, they hunted regularly, like other nobles. As knights, they would also go hawking. This involved using a trained hawk to catch prey and bring it back to the waiting knight (left).

CAN YOU RIDE A HORSE?

+ Equestrian skills essential

Learning to fight on horseback was the most important training for a young squire. At first, he used ponies for riding lessons. After much practice, a squire could control a horse while carrying weapons and wearing armor. He also learned to take care of horses. Warhorses took years to train. They learned how to wear armor and charge into battle (right).

❝ A squire should suffer himself … to learn to keep horse and learn to serve a knight, that he go with him to tourneys [tournaments] and battles. ❞

Medieval writer Ramon Lull on squires

Horses
Warhorses were chosen for their strength and aggression. In battle, the most powerful horses, called destriers, often fought and bit one another.

Knightly MVPs

In many societies, knights became heroes on and off the battlefield. They led large armies, defended borders, and conquered territory.

Did you know?

John Hawkwood fought for Edward III, but he spent most of his career as a mercenary. He fought in Italy for the cities of Pisa, Milan, and Florence. He became famous and rich.

SPANISH WARRIOR

+ El Cid in Spain...

+ ...fights on both sides!

Rodrigo Díaz de Vivar (right) was a Spanish military leader in the 1000s. He fought against the Islamic Moors who then ruled southern Spain. His skill on the battlefield earned him the nickname "El Cid," from an Arabic word meaning "lord." When the Spanish rulers sent him into exile, El Cid fought beside the Muslims. After a royal pardon, he returned to the Spanish side. He conquered Valencia and took over from his former Muslim **allies**.

SIR WILLIAM MARSHAL

✦ "The greatest knight that ever lived"

✦ Celebrated in poetry

After becoming a knight in France, William Marshal won fame by fighting in tournaments. He went on to serve under several kings, including Richard I of England, who gave him land and the title Earl of Pembroke. A poem was written about Marshal's achievements in battle, "The History of William the Marshal." At the time, such an honor was usually reserved for royalty. Marshal became the richest man in England and died at the age of 72.

NEWS FROM AFAR

Alexander Nevsky ruled the medieval Republic of Novgorod, a large territory in northern Russia. Nevsky defeated Swedish, Lithuanian, and German invasions. At the same time, he avoided conflict with the Mongol empire to the east. One of his most famous victories was the Battle on the Ice in 1242. Nevsky's men defeated the Teutonic Knights in a fight on a frozen river (left).

My Medieval Journal

Imagine you want to be a mercenary, like Sir John Hawkwood. Using evidence from this book, write a letter to a possible employer to persuade him to hire you. List the kinds of skills you think would be useful for a mercenary to possess.

THE KING'S MAN

- A French hero
- Bertrand makes his name

Bertrand du Guesclin (right) was King Charles V's second in command in France during the Hundred Years' War. Despite being defeated more than once, du Guesclin became a hero. He won several battles against the English and reclaimed territory for France. In 1366, du Guesclin hired an army of mercenaries. He helped win King Charles a crucial alliance with the Spanish King Henry II.

Statue!

Many medieval sculptors made statues of knights on horses. They could demonstrate their skill by having a statue's whole weight held up by just two thin horse legs.

Glossary

allies People who agree to act together to achieve a purpose

coat of arms An official design that identifies a person, a family, or a business

coronations Ceremonies at which a king or queen is crowned

courtly love A medieval tradition of telling stories about a knight's love for his lady, who is usually a married woman

Crusades A series of religious wars fought between Christians and Muslims for control of the Holy Land

dubbing Describes a ceremony related to naming

feudal system A social organization in which all land is held in return for service to a king or a lord

hierarchy A society or system in which people are ranked in order of importance

hospice A place providing care for the sick, especially people who are dying

idealized Represented as perfect, or better than reality

joust To fight on horseback with lances

longbows Long, powerful bows

mercenaries Hired soldiers who fight for foreign armies in return for pay

migration The large-scale movement of people to settle in new places

minstrels Musicians who sang poetry accompanied by music

nobles People who hold a high rank in a feudal society and pass it on to their family

oath A solemn promise

orders Societies of monks, nuns, or knights who live by the same rules of behavior

outlaw A person who has broken the law but has not yet been caught

pagans People who do not follow any of the major religions

pilgrims People who travel to sacred places for religious reasons

professional Doing a task as a paid occupation

romantic Idealized view of things

sieges Military operations in which positions are surrounded and forced to surrender

tournament A sporting meet in which knights competed at different events

truce An agreement to halt fighting

tunic A long, sleeveless shirt

vassals Holders of land in a feudal society

vows solemn promises

The feudal system emerges under Charles Martel in France.

Samurai knights become important in Japan.

The Knights Templar are founded to protect pilgrims in the Holy Land.

Eleanor of Aquitaine promotes the idea of courtly love at her court in France.

700s | **1095** | **1100s** | **1120** | **1136** | **1160s**

Pope Urban II summons the First Crusade. Knights travel to the Holy Land to fight.

European knights begin to use coats of arms to identify themselves when in armor.

First mention in literature of the legendary King Arthur.

On the Web

www.ducksters.com/history/middle_ages/history_of_knights.php

A page about how knights lived and fought in the Middle Ages.

www.dkfindout.com/uk/history/castles/knights/

An overview of a knight's life, with links to information about training, weapons, and warfare.

www.historyforkids.net/the-crusade.html

A History for Kids page that tells the story of the Crusades.

medievaleurope.mrdonn.org/chivalry.html

A description of the code of chivalry that medieval knights tried to follow.

www.yourchildlearns.com/heraldrygame/index.html

An online game based on medieval heraldry.

Books

Claybourne, Anna. *Knight Survival Guide* (Crabtree Connections). Crabtree Publishing, 2011.

Gravett, Christopher. *Knight* (DK Eyewitness). DK Children, 2015.

Hanel, Rachel. *Life as a Knight: An Interactive History Adventure* (You Choose: Warriors). Capstone Press, 2010.

Lee, Adrienne. *Knights* (Legendary Warriors). Capstone Press, 2013.

Macdonald, Fiona. *You Wouldn't Want to Be a Medieval Knight!: Armor You'd Rather Not Wear.* Turtleback, 2013.

Sutcliff, Rosemary. *The Sword and the Circle: King Arthur and the Knights of the Round Table.* Paw Prints, 2008.

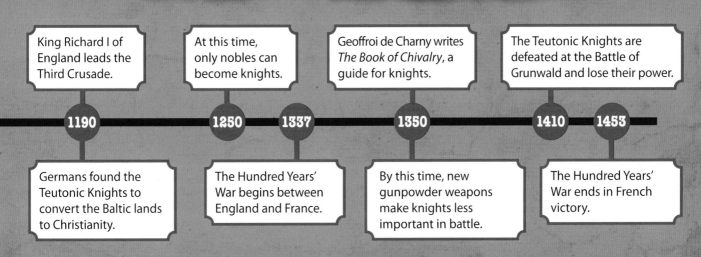

King Richard I of England leads the Third Crusade.

At this time, only nobles can become knights.

Geoffroi de Charny writes *The Book of Chivalry*, a guide for knights.

The Teutonic Knights are defeated at the Battle of Grunwald and lose their power.

1190   **1250**   **1337**   **1350**   **1410**   **1453**

Germans found the Teutonic Knights to convert the Baltic lands to Christianity.

The Hundred Years' War begins between England and France.

By this time, new gunpowder weapons make knights less important in battle.

The Hundred Years' War ends in French victory.

Index